FANNIE LOU
HAMER

and the
Fight for the Vote

by Penny Colman

GATEWAY CIVIL RIGHTS
THE MILLBROOK PRESS
BROOKFIELD, CONNECTICUT

TO MOLLY MURPHY MACGREGOR, A SEMINAL VOICE IN
THE TEACHING OF MULTICULTURAL WOMEN'S HISTORY

*SNCC workers organized the 1965 march
from Selma to Montgomery.*

Photographs courtesy of Magnum Photos: cover (Cornell
Capa), cover inset (Bruce Davidson), pp. 4 (Cornell Capa),
21 and 30 (Bruce Davidson), 24–25 (Danny Lyon); UPI/
Bettmann: pp. 1, 8, 26, 28; James H. Karales/Peter
Arnold Inc.: pp. 2–3; AP/Wide World Photos: pp. 6, 13;
Library of Congress: p. 11; Black Star: pp. 14 (Charles
Moore), 19 (Matt Herron); George Ballis/Take Stock,
Sausalito, CA: pp. 23, 29; Bernice Johnson Reagon: p.
27 (photo by Sharon Farmer).

Library of Congress Cataloging-in-Publication Data
Colman, Penny.
Fannie Lou Hamer and the fight for the vote
by Penny Colman.
p.   cm.—(Gateway civil rights)
Includes bibliographical references and index.
Summary: A biography of the civil rights activist who
devoted her life to helping blacks register to vote and
gain a national political voice.
ISBN 1-56294-323-5 (lib. bd.)
1. Hamer, Fannie Lou—Juvenile literature.   2. Afro-
Americans—Biography—Juvenile   literature.   3. Civil
rights workers—United States—Biography—Juvenile literature.   4. Afro-Americans—Suffrage—Mississippi—
Juvenile literature.   5. Afro-Americans—Civil rights—
Mississippi—Juvenile literature.   6. Civil rights move-
ments—Mississippi—History—20th   century—Juvenile
literature.   7. Mississippi—Race relations—Juvenile literature.   [1. Hamer, Fannie Lou.   2. Civil rights work-
workers. 3. Afro-Americans—Biography.] I. Title.
II. Series.

E185.97.H35C35   1993
973'.0496073'0092—dc20   [B]   92-21380   CIP   AC

Published by The Millbrook Press
2 Old New Milford Road, Brookfield, Connecticut 06804

On *August 22, 1964,* millions of Americans watched a black woman speaking on television. She was powerfully built and had a round face and wide shoulders. Her voice was strong and clear. Sometimes she spoke fast. Sometimes slow. Sometimes it sounded like she was singing. The woman's voice went right inside people and made them pay attention.

The woman was Fannie Lou Hamer. She was one of the cofounders and the vice-chair of the Mississippi Freedom Democratic Party (MFDP). Along with other members of the MFDP, Hamer had come to the Democratic National Convention in Atlantic City, New Jersey, as a delegate to select the Democratic candidate for president of the United States. But there was a big problem. Another group of people, called the Mississippi Regulars, had come, too. They claimed that they were the official delegates. The Regulars were white delegates who had been elected by the all-white Mississippi Democratic party. The MFDP had both black and white delegates who had been elected by both black and white voters in Mississippi.

According to the rules of the convention, the Credentials Committee would decide which group from Mississippi would be seated as official delegates. Well-known civil rights leaders testified before the committee. Martin Luther King, Jr., spoke.

During the 1964 Democratic National Convention, civil rights leaders protested that blacks had no voice in politics.

*The nation heard Fannie Lou Hamer speak for
the first time at the Democratic Convention.*

Then it was Fannie Lou Hamer's turn. She put her white purse down on the massive wooden table and sat down. Resting her arms on the table, she put her hands together with her fingers intertwined and started to speak.

"My name is Mrs. Fannie Lou Hamer and I live at 626 East Lafayette Avenue, Ruleville, Mississippi, Sunflower

County," she began. "If the Freedom Democratic party is not seated now, I question America. Is this America? The land of the free and the home of the brave? Where we have to sleep with our telephones off the hook, because our lives be threatened daily?" Her voice rang as clearly as a church bell.

Without notes, without hesitation, Fannie Lou Hamer continued. She described the terrors black citizens faced every day they lived in Mississippi. She talked about how black people lost their jobs and their homes if they tried to vote. How they were beaten. Arrested. Murdered. How three young civil rights workers—one black and two white—had been murdered that summer in Mississippi because they were fighting against segregation, the system that denied black people their rights as American citizens. And she talked about how she had been arrested and beaten the year before.

Fannie Lou Hamer's testimony shocked television viewers. The Credentials Committee received a deluge of calls and telegrams supporting the MFDP delegates. Finally the committee decided on a compromise proposal. Two MFDP delegates could be "at large" delegates, or unofficial participants at the convention. Fannie Lou Hamer was furious. She rejected the compromise, calling it "token rights, on the back row, the same as we got in Mississippi. We didn't come all this way for that mess again."

The Regulars did not like the compromise either because it required them to support the national Democratic party platform, which opposed segregation. In addition, the compromise said that no state delegations would be seated at future conventions unless *all* the registered Democrats of the state had been involved in selecting the delegates.

Most of the Regular Democrats refused to accept the compromise and left the convention.

The MFDP left, too. But not before Fannie Lou Hamer had made her point. Two nights in a row, she led the MFDP delegation onto the convention floor. She tried to get seated.

A wall of policemen blocked members of the Mississippi Freedom Democratic Party, led by MFDP head Aaron Henry and Fannie Lou Hamer, from entering the Democratic convention hall.

She talked to television reporters. She led the MFDP delegates in singing freedom songs like "Go tell it on the mountain over the hills and everywhere. Go tell it on the mountain to let my people go. . . ."

Each time guards removed them.

Finally Fannie Lou Hamer and the MFDP went back to Mississippi. For the rest of her life, Hamer fought to get black people to register and vote, to run for office, and to put an end to segregation.

"Life was worse than hard. It was horrible!"

Fannie Lou Hamer spent her whole life in Mississippi. She was born in a shack in Montgomery County on October 6, 1917. The youngest of twenty children, Fannie Lou had fourteen brothers and five sisters. Her parents, Jim and Lou Ella Townsend, were sharecroppers, or farmers who lived on land that someone else owned. Sharecroppers had to buy the seeds, fertilizer, and other supplies. Then they planted, weeded, and picked the crops. After all that, they had to "share," or give half of the crop to the landowner.

As an adult, Fannie Lou Hamer remembered her growing-up years: "Life was worse than hard. It was horrible! We never did have enough to eat and I don't remember how old I was before I got my first pair of shoes, but I was a big girl. Mama tried to keep our feet warm by wrapping them in rags and tying them with string.''

By the time she was six years old, Fannie Lou was in the fields with her family picking cotton. The older she got the more cotton she picked—thirty pounds a day, sixty pounds, then two to three hundred pounds. At one point, things got better for the Townsend family. They managed to save enough money to buy three mules, two cows, and some farm tools. ''We were getting along pretty well and my father even bought a car,'' Hamer later recalled.

But then a white neighbor poisoned their animals. ''He couldn't stand to see Negroes doing all right,'' Hamer explained. ''We went right back down to the bottom again, and that's where we stayed—right back sharecropping.''

Fannie Lou desperately wanted a ''real, good education.'' She got some, but not much. Sharecroppers' children could only go to school from December through March. The rest of the time they had to work in the fields. Then, when she was twelve years old, Fannie Lou had to quit school altogether. Terrible economic problems were sweeping America. The stock market crashed in October 1929, leading the country into the Great Depression. Fannie Lou had to stay home and help her family survive.

In the 1930s, life for sharecroppers in Mississippi was grim.

They survived by walking miles and miles through cotton fields looking for scraps of cotton left on a bush or lying on the ground. When they had scrapped enough cotton to make a bale, Lou Ella Townsend would sell it to buy some food. As Fannie Lou later remembered, a meal might be ''some corn-meal and an onion cut up with some salt on it, or maybe flour gravy.'' Lou Ella Townsend would also help people slaughter hogs and hope that they would give her the hog's intestines or the feet and head to take home and cook for her family.

Fannie Lou Hamer never forgot how hard she and her family worked. She also never forgot the lessons her mother taught them about dignity and self-respect.

As an adult, Hamer told this story, ''At the beginning of my young life, I wanted to be white. The reason was that we worked every day, hard work, and we never did have food. . . . I asked my mother one time why I wasn't white, so that we could have some food. She told me, 'Don't ever, ever say that again. Don't feel like that. We are not bad because we're black people. . . . You respect yourself as a black child. And when you're grown, if I'm dead and gone, you respect yourself as a black woman, and other people will respect you.' ''

''I was just curious to go, so I did.''

In 1944, when she was twenty-seven years old, Fannie Lou married Perry Hamer. Everyone called him Pap. He was a tractor driver and sharecropper on a plantation owned by W. D. Marlowe about four and a half miles outside of Ruleville, Mississippi. Fannie Lou Hamer had three jobs. She picked cotton. She was a timekeeper, which meant that she kept the records of how many bales each worker picked, and she cleaned Marlowe's house. She and Pap adopted two daughters, Dorothy Jean and Virgie Ree.

Fannie Lou Hamer worked hard from dawn to dark. The only time she sat down and rested was Sunday mornings, when she went to church. One Sunday morning, August 26, 1962, she listened to the preacher talk about a mass meeting that was going to be held at the church the following night. "Well, I didn't know what a mass meeting was, and I was just curious to go, so I did," Hamer later explained.

She discovered that it was a mass meeting about getting black people to register and vote that had been organized by two civil rights groups, the Southern Christian Leadership Conference (SCLC) and the Student Nonviolent Coordinating Committee (SNCC, pronounced SNICK).

Fannie Lou Hamer listened in amazement as James Bevel of SCLC and James Forman of SNCC talked about black people's right as American citizens to vote. "I heard it was our right as human beings to register and vote. I didn't know black people could vote. Nobody ever told me," she later said.

James Bevel of the Southern Christian Leadership Conference was one of the fiery speakers who set Hamer on the road of protest.

Volunteers trudged from house to house determined to help illiterate blacks fill out voter application forms and so claim this basic right as a citizen.

For years, white officials in Mississippi had been doing everything they could to prevent black people from voting—especially poor black people like Fannie Lou Hamer.

In order to vote, all Americans had to register. But in Mississippi before people could register they also had to pass a literacy test, which meant that they had to "read and interpret" the state constitution to the *satisfaction* of the registrar, or a white official who registered people. The registrar could also ask other questions. In one case a registrar asked a black man, "How many bubbles are there in a bar of soap?"

"If I don't answer this question I'm gonna flunk this test, ain't I?" the man replied.

"Yes, that's your question," said the registrar.

"Well, I don't want to be an ignorant man all the rest of my life . . . tell me how many bubbles are there in a bar of soap?"

Needless to say, the registrar got furious, and the man flunked the test.

After the literacy test, there was another obstacle—the poll tax, or a sum of money people had to pay before they could vote. Since most black people in Mississippi were very poor, they could rarely pay this tax.

If the literacy test and poll tax did not stop black people from voting, there was the Ku Klux Klan, a racist organization of white people who hid under white sheets and hoods and terrorized black people. And there was the Citizens Council, another racist organization that included prominent white politicians, doctors, lawyers, bankers, and real estate brokers who were determined to preserve segregation in Mississippi.

By 1960 only five percent of black people in Mississippi, or one out of every twenty, who were old enough to vote had been allowed to register.

Even before the meeting ended, Fannie Lou Hamer had made up her mind. When the leaders asked for volunteers to go to the courthouse in Indianola, Mississippi, she put up her hand. "I could just see me votin' people outa office I know was wrong," she said later. Hamer knew that going to Indianola could be dangerous, "but what was the point of being scared? The only thing they could do to me was kill me, and it seemed like they'd been tryin' to do that a little bit at a time ever since I could remember."

"I was tryin' to register for me."

On August 31, 1962, Hamer and seventeen other volunteers boarded an old yellow bus owned by a black man who agreed to drive the group to Indianola. As a group, they walked into the registrar's office. They filled out applications, and one by one, they took the literacy test. One by one, they all failed. According to Hamer, the registrar "asked me to copy and interpret part of the Mississippi Constitution. I could copy it, but I sure couldn't interpret it, for up to that time, I hadn't even known Mississippi had a constitution. We didn't learn nothin' about it in school." Hamer vowed to study the constitution until she could pass the test.

On the way back to Ruleville, the bus was stopped by state police officers who ordered everyone off the bus. A SNCC worker on the bus, Charles McLaurin, later described the scene: "Everybody on the bus was shaking with fear . . . then this voice singing church songs just came out of the crowd and began to calm everybody. . . . Somebody said, 'That's Fannie Lou, she know how to sing.' "

The police ordered the group to go back to Indianola. When they got there, the bus driver was arrested because the bus was the wrong color. It was too yellow. "Now ain't that ridiculous?'' Hamer said later. ''This same bus had been used for years to haul people to the cotton fields to pick cotton.''

The bus driver was fined one hundred dollars. No one in the group had that much money. Finally the fine was reduced to thirty dollars. According to Hamer, ''All of us *together*— not one, but all us together—had enough to pay.''

More trouble was waiting for Fannie Lou Hamer at home. The registrar had called her boss, W. D. Marlowe. That evening Marlowe told Fannie Lou Hamer, ''You'll have to go back to Indianola and withdraw [your application], or you have to leave this place.''

''Mr. Marlowe, I wasn't tryin' to register for you today. I was tryin' to register for me, '' Hamer said.

She left that night and went to Mr. and Mrs. Robert Tucker's home in Ruleville. Ten days later, sixteen bullets were fired into the Tucker home. Fannie Lou Hamer escaped to her niece's house in a town about forty miles away. Before long she returned to Ruleville. ''I was just sick of runnin' and hadn't done nothin','' Hamer later explained.

On December 3, 1962, Fannie Lou Hamer and her family moved into a run-down, three-room house without running water in Ruleville. Pap had lost his job for sticking by Fannie Lou. And no one would give him another one. Fannie Lou Hamer had lost her job. She had been shot at. Her family did not have any money, or furniture, or car. All this had happened because she wanted to vote.

On December 4, Fannie Lou Hamer went back to the courthouse in Indianola. This time Hamer told the registrar, "Now, you cain't have me fired 'cause I'm already fired, and I won't have to move now, because I'm not livin' in no white man's house. I'll be here every thirty days until I become a registered voter."

A month later, Fannie Lou Hamer passed the test. At last she was a registered voter. Now she had to save money to pay the poll tax. She also had to cope with white people who tried to scare her away. Night after night, men with guns drove slowly by her house. According to Hamer, "We would have to have our lights out before dark." But Fannie Lou Hamer refused to leave. "Why should I leave Mississippi," Hamer once told a reporter. "You don't run away from the problems, you just face them."

The first time Bob Moses, a leader of SNCC, met Fannie Lou Hamer, he realized that she was a born leader—a powerful grass-roots organizer. In 1963, Moses invited Hamer to attend the annual SNCC conference in Nashville, Tennessee. Before long, Fannie Lou Hamer was working for SNCC as a field secretary in Mississippi.

Hamer marched in a SNCC voter registration demonstration in Hattiesburg, Mississippi, 1963.

As she had all her life, Hamer worked from dawn to dark. This time, however, she was doing work she believed in. Work she was willing to risk everything for, including her life.

"You're under arrest."

On June 9, 1963, Fannie Lou Hamer and a group of other people were returning by bus to Mississippi after attending a voter-education workshop in Tennessee. When the bus stopped at the bus station in Winona, Mississippi, five of the people got off to get something to eat and use the bathroom. Fannie Lou stayed on the bus. When she saw her friends rush out of the bus station, Hamer got off the bus. Annelle Ponder told her that the police had ordered them out because the restaurant and bathroom were for white people only. Hamer got back on the bus. But when she saw the police shoving her friends into police cars, she got off again. "You're under arrest," a police officer told Hamer and kicked her as she got into his car.

From her jail cell, Hamer could hear the police beating Ponder. "They would call Annelle Ponder awful names . . . and I would hear when she would hit the floor . . . after awhile I saw Miss Ponder pass my cell. Her clothes had been ripped off from the shoulder down to the waist . . . Her mouth was swollen and bleeding. One of her eyes looked like blood."

Then the police came for Fannie Lou Hamer. They ordered two black male prisoners to beat her with a long, leather blackjack. First one beat her, then the other. "I began to scream, and one white man got up and began to beat me on my head and tell me to 'hush', " Hamer said.

Fannie Lou Hamer was beaten until her body was swollen and hard, her arms "had no feeling in them" and her hands "was as blue as anything you ever seen."

As soon as other civil rights workers heard about the arrests, they pressured the police into releasing Hamer and her friends, who then filed charges against the police. An all-white jury let the police go free.

Although Hamer never completely recovered from the beating, she did not stop her work. "Black people must register and vote," Hamer said over and over. She talked to black

During the march from Selma to Montgomery, blacks angrily demanded the vote. Soon after, the 1965 Voting Rights Act was passed.

people as they worked in the fields. She went to their shacks and their houses and churches. She spoke at mass meetings and led voter-registration workshops. She traveled to northern states to raise money for SNCC's programs. And despite having a pronounced limp because she had polio as a child, Hamer marched in civil rights demonstrations throughout the country.

Fannie Lou Hamer was blunt and outspoken. At one rally, she said, "Take a very close look at this American society. It's time to question these things . . . you always hear this long sob story that it takes time to change things. For three hundred years, we've given them time and I've been tired so long that I'm sick and tired of being sick and tired."

"This little light of mine."

Everywhere Fannie Lou Hamer went, she inspired people. One civil rights worker remembered being on a bus with Hamer after a voter-registration workshop. "People in the bus started worrying and getting pessimistic, saying things like, 'We can't do that. Nobody will follow us. Blacks won't stick together.' She [Fannie Lou Hamer] just started to sing. She was a spirit, an incredible spirit."

Another civil rights worker said that Fannie Lou Hamer was "one of the strongest people I have ever known. . . . She used to sing this song—'I've been 'buked [rebuked] and I've been scorned . . . But we'll never turn back, no, we'll never turn back, till we all are free.' "

Fannie Lou Hamer sang from deep inside herself. The power of her voice gave people hope and courage. She sang all the time, at mass meetings and in churches, at the Democratic National Convention, at protest meetings and demonstrations, and on long bus rides. Her favorite song was:

This little light of mine.
I'm going to let it shine,
Let it shine,
Let it shine,
Let it shine.

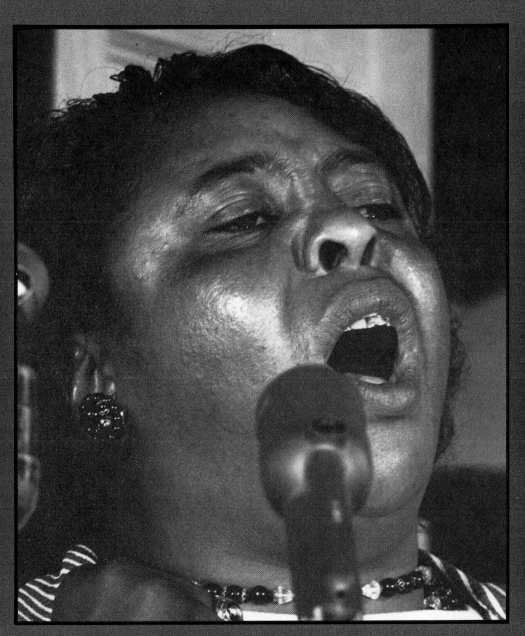

Fannie Lou Hamer used her powerful voice to sing about pain and faith.

FREEDOM SONGS

People in the civil rights movement sang. They sang all the time whether or not they had a good voice. They sang at mass meetings, during marches, demonstrations, and sit-ins, and in jail cells. Singing freedom songs made people feel strong and united. They sang freedom songs with titles such as "We Shall Overcome," "Over My Head I See Freedom in the Air," "We'll Never Turn Back," "Ain't A-Scared of-Your Jail," and "This Little Light of Mine." Some of the freedom songs were old church hymns or spirituals. Other freedom songs were new. The songs had messages in them about the importance of voting, praying, loving, supporting each other, and being brave. Sometimes singers would clap their hands. Or they would join hands and shout "Amen" or chant "Freedom Now!" Usually there was a song leader, or a person who would start each verse. Well-known song leaders included Cleo Kennedy, Sam Block, Mabel Hillary, and, of course, Fannie Lou Hamer.

Fannie Lou Hamer let her light shine all over America. In 1964 she ran for Congress. Although she lost, she won more than 33,000 votes. In 1968 the Democratic party held its national convention in Chicago. Fannie Lou Hamer was there again as a delegate from the Mississippi Loyalist Democratic Party (MLDP), a new party that had come out of the MFDP. Again the Regulars were there. Again there was a debate. This time the MLDP won. Fannie Lou Hamer took her seat and received a standing ovation. From 1968 to 1971 she was a member of the Democratic National Committee.

Hamer was a key speaker at the 1968 Democratic National Convention.

In 1969 Hamer bought forty acres of farmland in Mississippi and started the Freedom Farm Cooperative (FFC). Her dream was to build a community where poor people—black and white—could grow crops and build decent houses for themselves. "Hunger has no color line," she used to say. That same year, Fannie Lou Hamer received an honorary doctoral degree from Morehouse College along with Martin Luther King, Jr., and the vice president of the United States, Hubert Humphrey. In 1971 Hamer had raised enough money to buy another 640 acres for the FFC.

BERNICE REAGON

Bernice Reagon has a long list of accomplishments—singer, songwriter, scholar, researcher, founder of the popular singing group Sweet Honey in the Rock, and head of the Program in Black American Culture at the Smithsonian Institution's Museum of American History. In 1987 Reagon was awarded a MacArthur Fellowship, also known as the ''genius award.''

Thirty years ago, Reagon was a young woman and a singer with the SNCC Freedom Singers when she first met Fannie Lou Hamer. ''I was transformed,'' Reagon later recalled. ''As a young woman beginning to find my own voice, it was crucial that I sat in an environment created by the life and struggle of Fannie Lou Hamer.'' Years later Reagon wrote and recorded a powerful song about Hamer, ''Fannie Lou Hamer.''

And Hamer's light continued to shine. She was elected to the Central Committee of the National Women's Political Caucus. She taught a course in black history at Shaw University. She helped bring a factory to Ruleville where people could get jobs. She was involved in providing low-cost day-care centers and housing for poor people. Hamer's aim was "to support whatever is right, and to bring in justice where we've had so much injustice."

In 1976, white and black people together in Ruleville honored Hamer and celebrated "Fannie Lou Hamer Day."

The next year, on March 14, 1977, Fannie Lou Hamer died of cancer. She was fifty-nine years old. There were two

funerals for her in Ruleville, Mississippi. The first one was held at the Williams Chapel for her family and close friends. Later in the day, a memorial service was held at the Ruleville High School for dignitaries and ordinary people who came from all over Mississippi and America to honor her. At both services, there was lots of singing.

United Nations Ambassador Andrew Young spoke at Fannie Lou Hamer's funeral on March 20, 1977. "None of us would have been where we are now," he said, "had she not been there then."

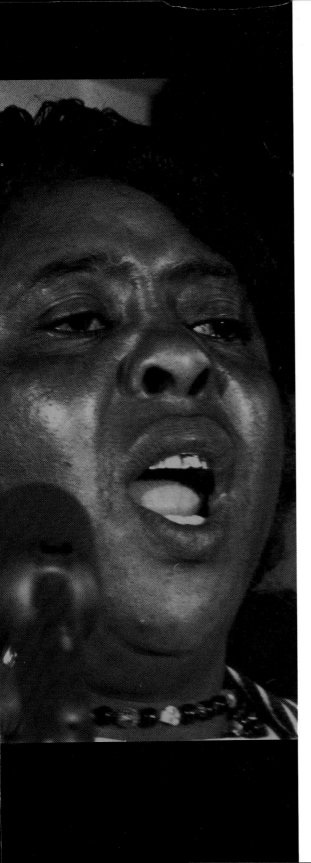

IMPORTANT EVENTS IN THE LIFE OF FANNIE LOU HAMER

1917	Fannie Lou Townsend is born in Montgomery County, Mississippi, on October 6.
1944	Fannie Lou marries Pap Hamer.
1962	Hamer goes to Indianola, Mississippi, to register to vote. Sixteen shots are fired at the home where she is staying.
1963	Hamer goes to work for the Student Nonviolent Coordinating Committee (SNCC). She is arrested and beaten in Winona.
1964	Hamer helps organize the Mississippi Freedom Democratic Party. She runs for Congress.
1968	Hamer is one of twenty-two delegates from Mississippi to be seated at the National Democratic Convention.
1969	Hamer starts the Freedom Farm Cooperative.
1971	Hamer is elected to the Central Committee of the National Women's Political Caucus.
1976	Hamer is honored in Ruleville on "Fannie Lou Hamer Day."
1977	On March 14, Hamer dies in Mound Bayou, Mississippi.

FIND OUT MORE ABOUT
FANNIE LOU HAMER

Videos: *Eyes on the Prize,* Episode 5, "Mississippi: Is This America?" for Hamer's appearance at the 1964 Democratic Convention (Boston: Blackside, 1987).

Women in the Movement (Washington, D.C.: WETA-TV, 1980).

Recordings: "Fannie Lou Hamer" by Bernice Johnson Reagon, recorded on *Sweet Honey in the Rock* (Emeryville, Cal.: Redwood Records, 1984).

Voice of the Civil Rights Movement, Black American Freedom Songs 1960-1966 (Washington, D.C.: Smithsonian Institution, Program in Black American Culture).

Book: *Fannie Lou Hamer* by June Jordan (New York: Crowell, 1972).

Poster: A poster of Hamer is distributed by the Organization for Equal Opportunity of the Sexes, P.O. Box 438, Blue Hill, ME, 04614.

INDEX